The Ultimate No-bake Cookbook

Delicious Dessert Recipes that You Don't Need To Bake!

Table of Contents

Introduction

A lot of people don't buy the idea of baking foods in the oven. They would rather have their goods prepared in a non-baked method.

When asked why, they said that during baking, a lot of nutrients are lost from the delicacies baked.

Come to think of it, this is very true because according to my research, I have noticed that the flavors and tastes of some ingredients are lost after baking.

So, I thought "how best can I enjoy some of my favorite baked goods without putting them through fire?", and I came up with no-bake versions of them.

Using the same ingredients but without baking them, I have learnt how to prepare most of my favorite desserts at home!

Now, it is your turn to learn how you can displace your oven and still enjoy delicious no-bake desserts in your home!

Turn the page and let's get started with the No-bake Nutella Cheesecake

No-Bake Cheesecakes

1. No-Bake Nutter Butter Cookie Cheesecake

Servings: 10-12 slices

Preparation Time: 1 hour

Chilling Time: 5 hours or overnight

The list of ingredients:

Crust:

- 1 tbsp. sugar
- 1/3 cup melted unsalted butter

- 24 pieces Nutter Butter cookies

Filling

- 8 pieces Nutter Butter cookies, broken into small pieces
- 2 cups heavy cream
- 1/4 cup confectioner's sugar
- 1 cup sugar
- 1 cup creamy peanut butter
- Thick chocolate syrup (for topping)
- 2 cups cream cheese, room temperature
- 2 cups frozen whipped topping (optional)
- 1 tsp vanilla extract

Methods:

For the crust:

Step 1

Using a food processor or by hand, finely crush the Nutter Butter cookies.

Step 2

Add the melted butter and sugar and continue to process until evenly mixed.

Step 3

Using the back of a spoon, carefully press the crust mixture onto the bottom of a 9-inch spring-form pan.

Step 4

Refrigerate crust for an hour.

For the filling:

Step 1

Beat the cream cheese, sugar, and peanut butter in a bowl using a mixer or by hand.

Step 2

In another mixing bowl, use a wire whisk to whip the heavy cream, vanilla extract, and confectioner's sugar until you can form stiff peaks.

Step 3

Fold in the cream cheese and Nutter Butter mixture into the whipped cream.

Step 4

Add the broken cookies and continue folding in until the cookies are evenly distributed.

Step 5

Take out the prepared crust from the refrigerator and fill it up with the mixture.

Step 6

Smoothen the top part of the cheesecake and refrigerate for 5 hours or overnight.

Step 7

Garnish with whipped cream and crushed cookies, drizzled with chocolate syrup before serving.

2. Easiest No-Bake Nutella Cheesecake

Servings: 6

Preparation Time: 15 minutes

Chilling Time: 4 hours

The list of ingredients:

- 1 cup semi-sweet chocolate chips
- 1 jar (13 oz.) Nutella spread

- 6 ready-made mini graham cracker pie crusts

- 2 cups cream cheese, at room temperature

- 1 cup white chocolate chips

- 1/2 cup confectioner's sugar

Methods:

Step 1

In a mixing bowl, combine Nutella, confectioners' sugar, and cream cheese.

Step 2

Fold in the ingredients or beat on low speed until you reach a smooth consistency.

Step 3

Carefully place the mixture into each mini graham crust.

Step 4

Melt the white chocolate chips in a double boiler until it turns into a thick liquid.

Step 5

Drizzle the melted white chocolate over the cheesecake mixture.

Step 6

Top with semi-sweet chocolate chips.

Step 7

Refrigerate the prepared cheesecakes and wait for at
least 4 hours before serving.

3. No-Bake Salted Caramel Cheesecake

Servings: 6-8 slices

Preparation Time: 20 minutes

Chilling Time: 5 hours or overnight

The list of ingredients:

For the caramel:

- 1/4 cup heavy cream
- 3/4 cup granulated sugar

- 1 tsp. salt
- 1/4 cup softened salted butter

For the cheesecake:

- 1 cup crushed graham crackers
- 1 tbsp. sugar
- 1 cup cream cheese
- 3/4 cup chilled heavy cream
- 1/4 cup salted butter

Methods:

For the caramel:

Step 1

Combine the ¾ cup sugar and salt in a saucepan. Melt over low heat while continuously stirring. You may add 4 Tbsp. water to avoid burning.

Step 2

When sugar and salt have melted, add the ¼ cup butter into the mixture and continue to stir.

Step 3

Add the heavy cream and continue stirring. Add 4 Tbsp. water if mixture starts getting lumpy.

Step 3

When everything has melted, remove from heat and
set aside to cool.

Crust:

Step 1

Mix the crushed graham crackers, ¼ cup butter, and
1 Tbsp. sugar.

Step 2

Press the mixture into a springform pan and
refrigerate.

Filling:

Step 1

In a separate bowl, whip the cream cheese and the
remaining heavy cream until fluffy.

Step 2

Add half of the salted caramel syrup.

Step 3

Mix until everything is evenly distributed.

Step 4

Add the remaining caramel syrup on top of the

cheesecake mixture.

Step 5

Refrigerate for 3- 4 hours.

Step 6

You may decorate with buttercream frosting or whipped cream before serving.

4. No-Bake Oreo Cheesecake

Servings: 8-10 slices

Preparation Time: 1 hour

Chilling Time: 5 hours or overnight

The list of ingredients:

Crust:

- 1/4 cup melted butter

- 1 154 g pack of Oreo classic cookies

Filling:

- 1 cup thick cream, whisked lightly
- 1/2 cup castor sugar
- 1/2 cup crumbled Oreo cookies
- 1 (1/4 oz.) packet of unflavored gelatin (2 ½ tsp), melted in ¼ cup boiling water
- 1/4 cup crushed Oreo cookies
- 1 tbsp. lemon juice
- 1 cup cream cheese

Methods:

For the crust:

Step 1

Crush the 154 g pack of Oreo classic cookies. You may use a food processor or a blender. The crushed cookies should have the consistency similar to that of moist soil.

Step 2

Mix the crushed cookies and butter.

Step 3

Use the back of a spoon to press the mixture onto a greased 8-inch spring-form cake pan for form a crust.

Step 4

Chill the prepared crust in the refrigerator while you prepare the cheesecake filling.

For the filling

Step 1

Using a mixer or a manual beater beat the sugar and cream cheese together until you achieve a smooth consistency.

Step 2

Add the lemon juice, gelatin mixture, and thick cream into the cream cheese mixture.

Step 3

Mix using a wooden spoon or a spatula until all ingredients of the filling are thoroughly combined.

Step 4

Add the crumbled cookies and mix evenly.

Step 5

Pour the filling mixture into the prepared crust mold.

Step 6

Smoothen the top part of the cheesecake and refrigerate the cake for 20 minutes.

Step 7

Take out the cake from the refrigerator and top with the crushed cookies.

Step 8

Refrigerate for 4-5 hours before serving.

No-Bake Fruity Desserts

5. No-Bake Tropical Rice Krispie Bars

Servings: 15-20 bars

Preparation Time: 20 minutes

Chilling Time: 2 hours

The list of ingredients:

Base:

- 1 tsp. coconut extract

- 1/3 cup macadamia nuts

- 6 cups puffed rice cereal or Rice Krispies

- 5 cups mini marshmallows

- 1/2 cup chopped dehydrated pineapple

- 1/2 cup white chocolate chips

- 1/2 cup chopped dehydrated guava

- 1/4 cup softened butter

Frosting:

- 1 ¼ cup cream of coconut

- 1/2 cup vegetable shortening

- 1 cup marshmallow creme

Topping:

- 1/2 cup sweet coconut flakes

Methods:

The Base:

Step 1

Place the marshmallows and butter in a saucepan.
Melt in low heat and keep stirring until everything

the two ingredients have melted completely.

Step 2

Turn off the heat and pour in the coconut extract. Stir until the extract has blended well with the mixture. Add the dehydrated fruits, rice cereal, nuts, and white chocolate chips. Mix until ingredients are evenly distributed.

Step 3

In a greased 9x13 baking pan, pour and spread the mixture evenly.

Step 4

Refrigerate to set.

The Frosting:

Step 1

Whisk all the frosting ingredients by hand or using a mixer with a whisk attachment. Whisk on medium speed. Increase speed little by little until it reaches fast speed. You will need to achieve a fluffy meringue-like consistency.

Step 2

Evenly spread the frosting over the pastry base.

The Topping and Final Step:

Step 1

In medium heat, toast the coconut flakes in a medium-sized wok and cook until the flakes turn golden brown. Stir the flakes continuously to keep them from burning.

Step 2

Wait for the coconuts flakes to cool then sprinkle them over the frosting.

Step 3

Refrigerate for 2 hours before serving.

6. Easy Millionaire's Pie

Servings: 6-8 slices

Preparation Time: 15 minutes

Chilling Time: Overnight

The list of ingredients:

- 1 ready-made graham cracker crust, or 6-8 ready-made graham mini crusts

- 1/3 cup lemon juice

- 1/2 cup mascarpone cheese, room temperature
- 1/2 cups chopped walnuts
- 1 tbsp. maraschino cherry juice
- 1 cup sweetened coconut flakes
- 1 ½ cups sweetened condensed milk
- 1/2 tsp. coconut extract
- 2 cups crushed pineapple, drained well to almost dry
- 2 cups freshly-whipped heavy cream

Methods:

Step 1

Combine coconut flakes, pineapple, walnuts, maraschino cherries, lemon juice, condensed milk, coconut extract, and cherry juice in a mixing bowl.

Step 2

In a separate bowl, whisk the whipped cream and mascarpone cheese until well-mixed, and you get a smooth consistency.

Step 3

Fold-in the first mixture into the whipped cream mixture until ingredients are evenly combined.

Step 4

Transfer the mixture into the crust or mini crusts.

Step 5

Refrigerate overnight.

Step 6

Garnish with a variations or combinations of these ingredients before serving: sweetened coconut flakes, whole maraschino cherries, pineapple, pecans, or silver or gold sugar pearls.

7. No-Bake Key Lime Pie

Servings: 6-8 slices

Preparation Time: 15 minutes

Chilling Time: 1 hour

The list of ingredients:

- 1/2 cup vanilla Greek yogurt
- 1 ready-made graham pie crust
- 3/5 cup sweetened condensed milk

- 1/3 cup key lime juice (or regular lime juice)
- Whipped cream for topping
- 1 cup cream cheese, room temperature
- Key lime slices, zested

Methods:

Step 1

Mix cream cheese, condensed milk, yogurt, and key lime juice in a mixing bowl until a smooth consistency is achieved. You may add one drop of green food coloring if you prefer a slightly richer lime color.

Step 2

Place the mixture into the ready-made graham crust.

Step 3

Refrigerate the pie for an hour.

Step 4

Before serving, top the pie with whipped topping.

Step 5

Use the lime slices and lime zest for garnish.

8. No-Bake Strawberry-Raspberry Cloud Cake

Servings: 6-8 slices

Preparation Time: 15 minutes

Chilling Time: Overnight

The list of ingredients:

- Chopped strawberries

- 1 cup cream cheese, room temperature

- 1 ½ cups confectioner's sugar

- 1 cup thawed frozen whip topping

- Ready-made graham crust

- 2 teaspoons blue raspberry flavored gelatin powder

- 1 cup strawberry preserves

Methods:

Step 1

In a mixing bowl, combine the whipped topping, cream cheese, and gelatin powder.

Step 2

Using an electric mixer with a paddle attachment, mix on high setting for about 5 minutes or until the gelatin has dissolved completely.

Step 3

Add the strawberry preserves and the confectioner's sugar. Continue to mix until completely and evenly distributed.

Step 4

Pour the mixture into the ready-made crust.

Step 5

Refrigerate overnight.

Step 6

Garnish with chopped strawberries before serving.

9. No-Bake Creamy Pineapple Cake

Servings: 8-10 slices

Preparation Time: 15 minutes

Chilling Time: overnight

The list of ingredients:

- 3/4 cup sweetened coconut flakes

- 1/2 cup lemon juice
- Maraschino cherries
- 2 ½ cups crushed pineapples
- 1 cup frozen whip topping, thawed
- 1 (11 oz.) box Mini Nilla wafers
- 1 2/3 cups sweetened condensed milk

Methods:

Step 1

Arrange a layer of wafers to cover the bottom of a 9-inch baking pan.

Step 2

In a mixing bowl, mix the pineapple, condensed milk, and lemon juice.

Step 3

Pour this mixture into the baking pan with wafers.

Step 4

Arrange more wafers on top of the fruit mixture.

Step 5

Top with whipped topping.

Step 6

Sprinkle flaked coconut on top.

Step 7

Refrigerate overnight.

Step 8

Top each slice with a cherry before serving.

10. Easy No-Bake Coconut Cream Pie

Servings: 6-8 slices

Preparation Time: 15 minutes

Chilling Time: 3 hours

The list of ingredients:

- 1 ready-made chocolate cookie pie crust/mini pie crusts

- 3/4 cup sweetened coconut flakes

- 1 cup thawed frozen whip topping
- 2 (3.4 oz.) packages of vanilla instant pudding mix
- 2 cups whole milk
- 1 tsp. pure coconut extract

Methods:

Step 1

Whisk the milk, pudding mix, and coconut in a large bowl for at least 2 minutes or until a smooth consistency is achieved.

Step 2

Add the whipped topping and coconut flakes into the mix and continue mixing.

Step 3

Refrigerate for 3 hours.

Step 4

For garnishing, you may use sweetened coconut flakes, sliced bananas, or sugar pearls.

Step 5

Serve cold.

Chocolate and Coffee

11. Mocha Icebox Cake

Servings: 6-8 slices

Preparation Time: 15 minutes

Chilling Time: Overnight

The list of ingredients:

- 2 cups heavy cream

- 34 pieces chocolate chip cookies (13 oz. pack of Chips Ahoy)

- 1 ready-made graham cracker crust
- 2 cups thawed frozen whip topping

Methods:

Step 1

Wet each cookie with the heavy cream and arrange each one to form a layer of cookies at the bottom of the crust.

Step 2

Cover the cookie layer with half of the whipped topping.

Step 3

Create another layer of cookies dipped in heavy cream and top it with another layer of whipped topping.

Step 4

Repeat this process for another layer.

Step 5

Top the pie with crushed cookies.

Step 6

Refrigerate overnight.

Step 7

Serve chilled.

12. No-Bake Chocolate Chip Cookie Pie

Servings: 6-8 slices

Preparation Time: 15 minutes

Chilling Time: Overnight

The list of ingredients:

- 2 cups heavy cream

- 34 pieces chocolate chip cookies (13 oz. pack of Chips Ahoy)
- 1 ready-made graham cracker crust
- 2 cups thawed frozen whip topping

Methods:

Step 1

Wet each cookie with the heavy cream and arrange each one to form a layer of cookies at the bottom of the crust.

Step 2

Cover the cookie layer with half of the whipped topping.

Step 3

Create another layer of cookies dipped in heavy cream and top it with another layer of whipped topping.

Step 4

Repeat this process for another layer.

Step 5

Top the pie with crushed cookies.

Step 6

Refrigerate overnight.

Step 7

Serve chilled.

13. No-Bake Espresso Choco Cookies

Servings: 36-40 cookies

Preparation Time: 20 minutes

Chilling time: 1 hours

The list of ingredients:

- 1/2 cup unsalted butter
- 1/2 cup mocha cappuccino hazelnut spread

- 1/2 tsp. instant espresso powder

- 2 cups sugar

- 1/2 cup fresh milk

- Pinch of kosher salt

- 3 cups quick cooking oats

- 1/4 cup unsweetened cocoa powder

Methods:

Step 1

Combine milk, sugar, cocoa powder, espresso powder, and butter in a saucepan and bring to a boil over medium heat.

Step 2

Keep boiling for 1 minute then remove from heat.

Step 3

Add oats, salt, and the hazelnut spread and mix thoroughly.

Step 4

Spoon mixture and drop onto a tray covered with parchment paper.

Step 5

Allow to cool in room temperature.

14. No-Bake Chocolate Tiramisu

Servings: 10-15 slices

Preparation Time: 15 minutes

Chilling Time: Overnight

The list of ingredients:

- 2 tbsp. cocoa powder

- 1/2 cup powdered sugar

- 1/2 cup coffee mixture (1 tsp coffee, 2 tbsps. sugar)

- 18 pieces chocolate flavored graham crackers
- 2 tbsp. sugar
- 1 cup chilled overnight heavy cream
- 1 cup cream cheese
- 1/2 cup water

Methods:

Step 1

Mix the black coffee and sugar in a bowl.

Step 2

In another bowl, whisk the cream cheese and add the powdered sugar until you achieve a fluffy consistency.

Step 3

In a separate bowl, whisk the heavy cream until it forms stiff peaks.

Step 4

Fold in the cheese mixture into the whipped cream until ingredients are combined evenly. Divide the mixture into three equal parts.

Step 5

Dip 6 graham cracker pieces in the coffee mixture and arrange them in a pan or a cake dish.

Step 6

Spread a layer of the cream mixture on the moist graham crackers.

Step 7

Repeat by doing two more layers of moist graham crackers and cream mixture.

Step 8

Chill overnight.

Step 9

Sift cocoa powder on top before serving.

15. French Silk Pie on Pretzel Crust

Servings: 6-8

Preparation Time: 20 minutes

Chilling Time: 2 hours

The list of ingredients:

For the pretzel crust:

- 1 ¾ cups crushed salted pretzels

- 1/4 cup honey

- 1/2 cup melted unsalted butter

For the pie filling

- 2 tsp. vanilla extract

Whipped topping:

- 1 ½ cups confectioner's sugar

- 2 tbsp. sour cream

- 1/2 cup softened unsalted butter

- Pinch kosher salt

- 1 tsp. espresso powder

Methods:

For the crust:

Step 1

Grease a 9-inch pie pan.

Step 2

Mix melted butter and honey in a bowl.

Step 3

Add the crushed pretzels and continue mixing until evenly combined.

Step 4

Firmly press the mixture onto the sides and bottom
of the greased pan.

Step 5

Refrigerate.

For the Filling:

Step 1

In a large bowl, mix the butter and confectioner's
sugar until it turns fluffy. If using an electric mixer,
mix for around 3 minutes.

Step 2

Add to the mixture the salt, sour cream, melted
chocolate, vanilla extract, and espresso powder.
Combine until evenly mixed and smooth.

Step 3

Transfer the filling into the pie crust and refrigerate
for another hour or two.

Step 4

Top with whipped topping before serving.

Candies

16. Peanut Brittle

Servings: 10 servings

Preparation Time: 15 minutes

Chilling Time: 1 hour

The list of ingredients:

- 1 tbsp. corn syrup

- 1/2 cup salted butter

- 1/2 cup sugar

- 2 cups cracked peanuts

Methods:

Step 1

Line a 9x 13 baking tray with parchment paper.

Step 2

Combine the sugar and butter in a large saucepan.

Step 3

Cook over medium heat while stirring continuously until fully melted and evenly mixed.

Step 4

Add the corn syrup and continue stirring for another 5 minutes until the syrup turns golden brown.

Step 5

Reduce the heat.

Step 6

Add the peanuts and stir until peanuts are evenly distributed.

Step 7

Pour this mixture over the lined baking tray. Make sure the syrups are flattened evenly.

Step 8

Cool in room temperature.

Step 9

Refrigerate for another hour.

Step 10

Break the peanut brittle in small pieces.

Step 11

Transfer to a jar or serve.

17. No-Bake Walnut Fudge Cubes

Servings: 15-18 pieces

Preparation Time: 5 minutes

Chilling Time: 1 hour

The list of ingredients:

- 1 cup chopped roasted walnuts
- 1 ½ cups semisweet chocolate chips

- 1 tsp vanilla extract

- 1 ¾ cup sweetened condensed milk

Methods:

Step 1

Prepare a baking tray lined with parchment paper.

Step 2

Combine the chocolate chips, condensed milk, and vanilla in a microwave-safe bowl.

Step 3

Microwave the above ingredients on high for 1 minute.

Step 4

Stir the mixture and add the chopped walnuts until ingredients are thoroughly mixed.

Step 5

Pour the mixture onto the baking tray with parchment paper and spread it out evenly.

Step 6

Refrigerate for an hour.

Step 7

Cut into small squares before serving.

18. No-Bake Peanut Butter Fudge Squares

Servings: 16 squares

Preparation Time: 15 minutes

Chilling Time: 4 hours

The list of ingredients:

- 1 ¾ cup (14-ounce can) condensed milk

- 1 ½ cup (12-ounce bag) peanut butter chips

- 2 tbsp. vanilla extract

- 1 ½ cup (12-ounce bag) semisweet chocolate chips

- 2 tbsp. unsalted butter

Methods:

Step 1

Line a baking dish (8x8 preferred) with parchment paper.

Step 2

Place the condensed milk, peanut butter chips, 1 Tbsp. butter, 1 tsp vanilla in a large microwave-safe bowl.

Step 3

Melt the above ingredients in a microwave oven on 50% power for 30 seconds. Mix the ingredients, return to the microwave, and repeat the procedure every 30 seconds until everything has fully melted.

Step 4

In a separate microwave-safe bowl, combine the chocolate chips, the rest of the condensed milk, 1 Tbsp. butter, and 1 tsp vanilla.

Step 5

Melt these ingredients in a microwave oven on 50% power for 30 seconds. Mix the ingredients, return to the microwave, and repeat the procedure every 30 seconds until everything has fully melted.

Step 6

Evenly spread the peanut butter mixture on the baking sheet at about half an inch thick. Spread the chocolate fudge on top.

Step 7

Using a knife, create swirl patterns on the peanut butter and chocolate fudge combination.

Step 8

Refrigerate for 4 hours.

Step 9

Cut the fudge into equal squares before serving.

19. Gummy Bears

Yield: 40 pieces

Preparation Time: 15 minutes

Chilling Time: 2 hours

The list of ingredients:

- 1 tbsp. lemon juice
- 1 cup of any fruit juice flavor

- Gummy bear molds

- 3 tbsp. unflavored gelatin granules (or 3 (.25 oz.) packets)

- 1/4 tsp. sugar

Methods:

Step 1

Boil the fruit juice in a saucepan.

Step 2

Add the gelatin to the boiling juice.

Step 3

Stir continuously for 3 minutes.

Step 4

Turn off the heat and add the sugar.

Step 5

Continue stirring until sugar is completely dissolved.

Step 6

Pour this mixture into the molds.

Step 7

Cool at room temperature, then refrigerate for at least 2 hours.

20. Sea Salt Caramel Candies

Servings: 60 candies

Preparation Time: 15 minutes

Cooking time: 30 minutes

Chilling Time: 2 hours

The list of ingredients:

- 1 cup corn syrup

- 2 cups light brown sugar, firmly packed
- 1 pinch sea salt
- 1/4 cup bourbon
- 1 tbsp. vanilla extract
- 1 cup white granulated sugar
- 1 cup salted butter
- Other items needed:
- Clear cellophane wrapper
- Candy thermometer

Methods:

Step 1

Line a baking tray with parchment paper.

Step 2

In a medium saucepan, place the cream, sugar, butter, bourbon, and corn syrup, then mix well.

Step 3

Attach a candy thermometer to the saucepan.

Step 4

Cook the ingredients over medium heat and simmer until the thermometer reaches 250°F.

Step 5

Add the salt and vanilla extract and continue cooking for 2 more minutes.

Step 6

Pour the mixture onto the baking sheet.

Step 7

Refrigerate for 2 hours.

Step 8

Transfer the caramel mixture from the tray to a cutting board.

Step 9

Using a knife sprayed with cooking spray, cut the caramel into 1-inch squares.

Step 10

Cut the cellophane wrappers into 4-inch squares.

Step 11

Wrap each square by rolling the caramel on each wrapper starting from the side. Twist the ends. Repeat until all pieces are wrapped.

Dessert Balls

21. Choco Cornflake Balls

Servings: 20 servings

Preparation Time: 20 minutes

Chilling Time: 10 minutes

The list of ingredients:

- 2 cups semi-sweet chocolate chips
- Candy sprinkles (for toppings)
- 4 cups regular corn flakes

Methods:

Step 1

Melt the chocolate chips in a double boiler or a microwave oven.

Step 2

Place the cornflakes in a large mixing bowl.

Step 3

Pour half of the melted chocolate into the cornflakes

Step 4

Using a rubber spatula, mix the ingredients until all cornflakes are completely coated.

Step 5

Wait for the chocolate to set, then pour the remaining melted chocolate into the flakes for a second coat.

Step 6

Quickly scoop the chocolate-coated cornflakes and form into a small mound onto a lined baking sheet. Work quickly before the chocolate hardens.

Step 7

Top with candy sprinkles.

Step 8

Refrigerate for not more than 10 minutes.

Step 9

Remove from the refrigerator and store in a dry, air-tight container. You can store this at room temperature for up to two weeks.

22. No-Bake Cookie Dough Brownie Balls

Servings: 48 balls

Preparation Time: 45 minutes

Chilling Time: 30 minutes

The list of ingredients:

- 1/4 cup granulated sugar

- 1 tsp. coconut oil

- 1/2 cup softened unsalted butter

- 3/4 cup mini chocolate chips

- 1/3 cup cream cheese

- 1 ¼ cups all-purpose flour

- 1/2 cup light brown sugar, firmly packed

- 1/2 cup creamy peanut butter

- 3 cups milk chocolate chips (semisweet version will also work)

- 2 tsp. vanilla extract

- 1 cup instant chocolate frosting

- 1/4 tsp. salt

- 1 (18.3-ounce) box brownie mix

Methods:

Step 1

In a large mixing bowl, beat the butter and brown sugar.

Step 2

Add the peanut butter, cream cheese, and sugar. Continue to beat the ingredients.

Step 3

Add the baking soda, vanilla, flour, and salt. Continue beating until thoroughly combined.

Step 4

Form the cookie dough into 48 small balls.

Step 5

Following the package directions, prepare the brownie mix. Allow to cool down completely, then crumble it into a bowl.

Step 6

Add the frosting and mix well.

Step 7

Coat each cookie dough with the brownie mixture by rolling. Form each one into a ball.

Step 8

Arrange each on one on a baking sheet lined with parchment paper.

Step 9

Refrigerate the balls.

Step 10

In a microwave-safe bowl, combine the chocolate chips and coconut oil.

Step 11

Heat in microwave oven for 30 seconds on High, stir, then heat in microwave oven again for a series of 15 seconds heating and mixing until the chocolate has thoroughly melted.

Step 12

    With a toothpick as a handle, dip each ball into the
    melted chocolate and return to the baking sheet.

Step 13

    Sprinkle each ball with mini chocolates.

Step 14

    Chill for 10 minutes before serving.

23. Funfetti Cake Batter Balls

Servings: 30 balls

Preparation Time: 30 minutes

Chilling Time: 30 minutes

The list of ingredients:

- 16 oz. white chocolate melting wafers
- 1 ½ cups Funfetti cake mix

- 1/4 cup rainbow nonpareils

- 1/2 cup all-purpose flour

- 2 tsp. vanilla extract

- 1/2 cup softened unsalted butter

- Rainbow nonpareils, chopped nuts, or coconut

- 1/2 cup sugar

Methods:

Step 1

Line a baking tray with parchment paper.

Step 2

Mix the cake mix, butter, sugar, vanilla, and flour in a food processor. Process the ingredients until a firm dough is formed. Transfer the mixture into another bowl.

Step 3

Add the ¼ cup of rainbow nonpareils into the dough mixture. Mix until evenly distributed.

Step 4

Form 1-inch balls from the dough and arrange them on the lined baking tray.

Step 5

Freeze the balls of dough for 10 minutes.

Step 6

Place the white chocolate in a microwave-safe bowl and melt them on 50% power in a series of 30-second routines of melting and stirring until the white chocolate has fully melted.

Step 7

Using a fork, dip each cake ball into the melted white chocolate. Remove from the fork and arrange on the baking tray.

Step 8

Sprinkle with nuts, coconut, or nonpareils.

Step 9

Refrigerate for 20 minutes before serving.

24. Pumpkin Cheesecake Balls

Servings: 16 balls

Preparation Time: 20 minutes

Chilling Time: 1 ½ hours

The list of ingredients:

- 3/4 cream cheese, at room temperature
- 1/2 cup milk

- 1/2 cup pure pumpkin puree

- 3/4 cup graham cracker crumbs

- 1 tsp. pumpkin pie spice

- 1/4 cup confectioner's sugar

- Candy toppings (optional)

- 2 ¼ white chocolate melting wafers

Methods:

Step 1

Prepare a baking sheet lined with parchment paper.

Step 2

Place the white chocolate in a microwave-safe bowl and melt in microwave oven on 50% power for a series of 30 seconds melting and stirring until the white chocolate has thoroughly melted.

Step 3

Mix the pumpkin puree, cookie crumbs, cream cheese, confectioner's sugar, and pumpkin spice in a bowl using an electric mixer with paddle on medium speed for 2 minutes. If using a hand mixer, mix on High for 2 minutes making sure to scrape the sides of the bowl occasionally.

Step 4

Add ½ cup of melted white chocolate into the
mixture and mix for another 2 minutes.

Step 5

Cover the bowl with cling wrap and refrigerate for 30
minutes.

Step 6

Form balls using a spoon or a ball-shaped scooper
and place them on the baking sheet lined with
parchment paper. Be careful to keep all edges
smooth.

Step 7

Freeze the balls for 1 hour.

Step 8

Reheat the white chocolate on High setting in the
microwave oven for 1 minute.

Step 9

Dip each ball into the melted chocolate until fully
coated. Use a dessert fork to handle the balls from
dipping to the baking sheet. Repeat the procedure
until all balls are coated with milk chocolate.

Step 10

Freeze until hardened.

Step 11

Top with candies, chocolate syrup, or whatever you want.

Step 12

Chill and serve chilled.

No-Bake Bars

25. No-Bake Choco Oatmeal Bars

Servings: 16-20 bars

Preparation Time: 15 minutes

Chilling Time: 4 hours

The list of ingredients:

- 1 cup dark chocolate chips
- 1 tsp. pure vanilla extract

- 1/2 cup packed brown sugar

- 1/4 tsp ground cinnamon

- 1 cup unsalted butter

- 3/4 cup chunky peanut butter

- 3 cups rolled oats

- 1/4 tsp. kosher salt

Methods:

Step 1

Line an 8x8 baking dish with parchment paper. Set aside.

Step 2

Combine, brown sugar, butter, and vanilla extract in a medium saucepan. On low heat, heat until the butter and sugar has completely dissolved.

Step 3

Add the cinnamon, oats, and kosher salt. Continue cooking while constantly stirring for about 5 minutes.

Step 4

Place half of the oatmeal mixture into the lined baking dish and spread it evenly while pressing down. Set aside.

Step 5

Combine the peanut butter and chocolate chips in a microwave-safe bowl. Heat in the microwave oven on High for 40 seconds. Remove from oven and stir. Return the mixture to the oven and repeat the procedure for a few more cycles of heating and stirring until the chocolate has fully melted.

Step 6

Pour ¾ of the melted chocolate mixture into the pan with pressed oats.

Step 7

Pour the remaining oat mixture and spread it evenly.

Step 8

Drizzle the remaining melted chocolate over the mixture.

Step 9

Chill in the refrigerator for 4 hours.

26. No-Bake Peanut Butter Bars

Servings: 12-16 bars

Preparation Time: 15 minutes

Chilling Time: 4 hours

The list of ingredients:

- 1 cup confectioner's sugar
- 1 cup creamy peanut butter

- 1/2 cup peanut butter chips, and some extra for toppings
- 1/2 cup melted unsalted butter
- 1/2 cup semisweet chocolate chips
- 1 cup graham cracker crumbs

Methods:

Step 1

Line an 8x8 baking dish with parchment paper.

Step 2

Combine the melted butter, graham cracker crumbs, and powdered sugar in a bowl.

Step 3

Add the peanut butter to the mixture and stir until evenly distributed.

Step 4

Pour the mixture into the prepared baking dish.

Step 5

Combine the semisweet chocolate chips and ½ cup of peanut butter in a microwaveable bowl. Place in the microwave oven to melt on 50% power for 30 seconds. Remove from oven and stir. Repeat procedure for several times until all the chocolate chips have melted.

Step 6

Pour the melted chocolate over the peanut butter mixture.

Step 7

Refrigerate for 4 hours.

Step 8

Cut into squares and serve.

27. Nutella Bars

Servings: 12-16 bars

Preparation Time: 15 minutes

Chilling Time: 30 minutes

The list of ingredients:

- 1 tsp. vanilla extract

- 2 cups sugar

- 1/4 cup creamy peanut butter

- 3 cups quick cook oatmeal

- 1/4 cup unsweetened cocoa powder

- 1/2 cup whole milk

- 1/8 tsp. kosher salt

- 1/4 cup Nutella

- 1/2 cup unsalted butter

Methods:

Step 1

Take a 9x13 baking dish and line it with parchment paper.

Step 2

Combine milk, sugar, cocoa powder, and butter in a saucepan. Stir while on medium heat on the stovetop. Boil for 1 minute.

Step 3

Remove from heat and add the Nutella, peanut butter, oatmeal, salt, and vanilla. Mix well.

Step 4

Transfer the mixture into the baking dish and press.

Step 5

Chill for 3 hours.

Step 6

Slice into bars before serving.

Spooned and Scooped Desserts

28. Strawberry Shortcake in a Jar

Servings: 2 shortcakes

Preparation Time: 5 minutes

Cooking time: 1 hour

The list of ingredients:

- 1 cup thawed whipped topping
- 1/2 cup sliced strawberries
- 2 mason mugs

- 6 mini vanilla wafer cookies

Methods:

Step 1

Arrange 3 vanilla wafers at the bottom of each mason mug.

Step 2

Add a quarter of the whipped topping to each of the mugs.

Step 3

Equally divide the strawberries and make a layer of strawberries and whipped topping.

Step 4

Create another layer of strawberries and the remaining topping.

Step 5

Refrigerate for 1 hour before serving.

29. S'mores in a Jar

Servings: 2 s'mores jars

Preparation Time: 5 minutes

The list of ingredients:

- Chocolate syrup
- 2 (3.25 oz.) containers Snack Pack instant chocolate pudding
- 6 pieces crushed graham crackers

- 1 cup mini marshmallows

Methods:

Step 1

Divide the ingredients into 2 equal parts.

Step 2

Arrange the graham cracker crumbs, chocolate pudding, and mini marshmallows in layers.

Step 3

Top with chocolate syrup and serve.

30. Slow Cooker Brownie Pudding

Servings: 6-8

Preparation Time: 15 minutes

Cooking time: 2-3 hours

The list of ingredients:

- 2 cups whole milk
- 1 package (3.9 oz.) Jello chocolate pudding mix
- 1/2 tsp. instant espresso powder

- 2 ¼ cups (18 oz. box) brownie mix

- 1/4 cup semisweet chocolate chips

- Ice cream for topping

Methods:

Step 1

Coat a 6-quart slow cooker with cooking spray.

Step 2

Prepare the brownie mix following the package instructions.

Step 3

Transfer the brownie batter to the slow cooker.

Step 4

Top with chocolate chips.

Step 5

In a separate bowl, whisk the pudding mix, milk, and espresso powder.

Step 6

Pour the pudding mixture onto the brownie mix.

Step 7

Place a paper towel securely before closing the lid so that the condensation won't fall on the batter.

Step 8

Cook on High setting for 2-3 hours.

Step 9

Check after 2 hours to see if the edges have separated
from the insert.

Step 10

The pudding will still appear wet, but this is just
normal.

Step 11

Scoop into mugs or saucers.

Step 12

Top with ice cream before serving.